Of: Vol. I

Ossian Foley

UDP

ISBN 978-1-937027-22-3
First Edition, First Printing

Ugly Duckling Presse
232 Third Street, #E303
Brooklyn, NY 11215
uglyducklingpresse.org

Distributed by SPD/Small Press Distribution
1341 Seventh Street
Berkeley, CA 94710
spdbooks.org

Design by Carly Dashiell and Ossian Foley
in Franklin Gothic Book and Avenir
Books printed on recycled paper
and bound at McNaughton & Gunn

Hasse Diagram of powerset of {x, y, z} by KSmrq is licensed
under a Creative Commons Attribution-Share Alike 3.0 Unported
License.

Support for this publication was provided by the National
Endowment for the Arts.

Of: Vol. I

Table of Contents

gather in
       the presences
summer time and the living—

s/t, where I ≥

let us change Nature
by flame
       of time to frolic

for the mantic
        'tis no use
which gives us
       a law

dissipates—an imprint
persists—a shallow sea

still
   storms hunt the sky

ever so
          reaching
for to
          ward a way
off oft out in
                    the
distant present ever
so
     becoming

bestow to power more
over power to matter
ought be cause my brain
~s all the way down

immense ballast
                 taut
against calm winds naught
inchartable
            whence
you go there you are
so
    whether to lee of

$$\frac{1}{20}$$

precipitate inform
nature bechance
                    return
nurture hast
            disclosed
prim- and coordial
a member of
                the cloud
out from nor
            goodly rite

$\frac{1}{15}$

novelty if not—this
somehow shall affirm—this
reproducible—this

nature borne by those
                        tho'
implosion or impulsion

all incident upon—

$$\frac{1}{12}$$

cur rent a light on ward
awave from
                whenceforth
measure of
            to divine
interherence
                who
some how inversely Ω

$$\frac{1}{10}$$

all is signal all is noise
signal descry identity
with the identified
                  speak
with the spirits and
                      forget
failure modes
              skepticism
which affirms which is
                      to say
perhaps as to that yes
                    please
failure modes
            in the noise was
the signal and the signal
was with identity

inaction incarnate
precede me
            like this
weather we've been
having been

$$\frac{2}{15}$$

if found

       often
certain passes
alone

      perhaps

deep
    and common
time and
      descent

$$\frac{3}{20}$$

timber once umber
then
        umber again
buries in amber
again
        the whole wood

leaves millions of these
nought
            we claim what light
cooling shapes
                    scatter
off on wind in wind

$\frac{1}{6}$

though the trajectory

till till regress like that
sound nestles
                somersaults
the wound
            spring bound withoutward
winters the
                fell away

of the whether
                or not

$$\frac{11}{60}$$

funny little animal
not garden universe
death thoughed
                hermitage

diffusion whereso we may
mingle
          autumns then leaves
as everything

$$\frac{1}{5}$$

        still sense
caducous
        keepsake like
a phantom
        encounter
the wild
        the whiledest
mutation
        the mutation
as everything

deflates withoutward

a difficult way
to
    say I have friends

and sorrows
                congregate

we care for those who
care for those who we

and mournings shine

phylogeny
            of grief

myth of phenotypes

a tribal mimicry

or disparate times

I shall rest in this place

nor chaos as such

$$\frac{1}{4}$$

of small and panic
like a
          radicate
lave
        conform the whorl
or contain the whorl
radiant
            as if

$$\frac{4}{15}$$

tripst of waking
waking over
some shore some hour

away
        the whiles

nigh
        night abeam
nigh a glimmer
the sealess

                asail

$$\frac{17}{60}$$

souse with spray
               —yet awash
in rimless floods the boundless
touch
      hand in hand without
halt
    the sail spans the bay
bent to
      time at bay

$\frac{3}{10}$

down to
          ghost of
matter

          the dust
idols of mean

mists
          thrice reclaim
among

          them flotsam
tauten
          so

$\frac{19}{60}$

epiprophetic of

the multitude
                proximate
to to start
            the world that is

anew anew incant
amidst
          the brilliance

that is
          no death only death

$$\frac{1}{3}$$

these wandering abstain
of wonders daunt
                        nor

convey thither trough
                        sea

shores our days
                neither
crest
        grave yet we recede

$\dfrac{7}{20}$

the organism

the single self

spans life spans

tho' senescence

always conceiving

$$\frac{11}{30}$$

whither
      thus at dawn

echo of
      absence
of

  symptoms, briefly

in here it inheres

and yet the tortoise

$\frac{23}{60}$

sex and death

...

toward a heaven

...

no wonder

...

$$\frac{2}{5}$$

and yet the tortoise

echoes
            the ghost of us

echoes
            the mortal fuss

$$\frac{5}{12}$$

thus perturbations
of matter
               thus
deformations form
beasts
          emergent
shadows in some
                      sense
lit within
             finite
totem like though

effaced so quickened
so open so bright

beast there is more
a thousand things

strings   vibrations
out of darkness
strings   pitch   light

all along we've been
uncertain
               now we
see the electron

totem of things known so
so all the more frightening

not a body anumber of
shadows in some sense
                          light without

beasts of this earth
                        annihilate
with those who would with you
annihilate
            o beasts your twin

7/15

all over hands
all over caves
covered in hands
all over caves

absolutely cavernous
atonelly resound

I thee rock inhere
I thee rock shroud

Δ

I have no ancestors
I am always afraid

transparent in that without
information
                mean of
a pane
        division fleet yet
vicious in the finite
nearness
                of the crisis
inexorably ancient
literally cannot give

$$\frac{1}{2}$$

humble - that - which is right

often mingled with pain
the everywhere spirit

surely would cause this to be

$$\frac{31}{60}$$

heart is crossroads
is death

         fond of
children follow

for ever in return

$$\frac{8}{15}$$

want of conveyance

carried over from
some ancestral route

hurry my children
let us not fall

to think distant thoughts

$\frac{11}{20}$

threat upon horseback
threat upon threat
                    nigh
and more nigh yet

thither
        all ways

noise in the mourning
oft just
        a little
dissolution

a kind of kind

17
—
30

love
and do
what
you will~
we will
do
we will
hear

א

it follows
that disfigure
it I have
said before
before pulsing
set
all of

Alef is number one. ¶ However the one that is referred to is "one not in counting" as the Tikkuney Zohar says. ¶ That means that alef represents something more than just a 'one thing', as opposed to nothing or two things. ¶ It represents wholeness, unity, cohesiveness, continuity, singularity. ¶ The way I understand this is that unity must include everything that is as well as everything that is not if it is indeed unity. All possibility as well as all actuality. Past, future, and present...etc... ¶ So I understand alef to include zero. One, as a number, is not infinity. It is being and existence. It excludes non-being and non-existence. So I can only conclude that alef must be represented by the equation $0=1$. That is comprehensive and whole, considering the '1' is everything (in conventional language) and '0' is nothing. If there is a true unity that encompasses all nothing and everything must be a single continuum that goes beyond division. Thus alef is $0=1$.
—David Chaim Smith, personal correspondence

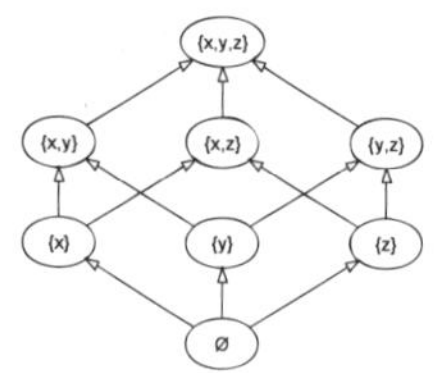

each one a lone
limits of sorts

perfect doom
diminishing

returns to space
abandon

all abandon

OHM and not OHM
and not not WHO

does much kindness
to be come last

$$\frac{3}{5}$$

to watch to awake
a waking of a

surface disturbance

known only whence nor
rate nor position

only direction

$$\frac{37}{60}$$

awe before grandeur

instant and utter
awe before absence

whose center holds

$\frac{19}{30}$

incidental
in its essence
to the child's
small universe
there may appear
an element
of marvel of
self
    surrender

$\frac{13}{20}$

in the brain a brain
saying here's a voice

you too will enter that realm
of maybe-help-maybe-hurt

the Territory
and the Adventure

Δ

All are my relations
I am always afraid

$\frac{2}{3}$

mooring pulse of

does us some
                good
the feeling does

somesuch
            matter
as we are
            the times

upon the bay

wholly patience
            wholly
every thing
            through idleness
the earth will see you
                  through
void forms
            life but one life of

change
        the absence of
the wind rises the wind dies
winds all ways about

uncertainly a low
probability event

the oracle which is

all possible
                 furies
worms every one
                      offers

which offering to which
too massive to support

every beast as such
slight divergence as I

someone else must tell you

43
—
60

it is all so

impossible

places
wrong the
all in
cause for
looking

the work
            that doing
needs
            cannot be

11
—
15

a wave
        through which
potential which

displaces
        designs
emerges
        in sum

all ways disclose
all past
        sounding

$$\frac{3}{4}$$

of perfect measure to
solve the whole
              story of
waking along time
               some
where any way in time
we wait what is feeling me

$$\frac{23}{30}$$

laws in the dark

the dark
          of men
a particular
kind of
          another

encoded in
               so

slight
          the meekest
the mere
               presence
of another
               source

that it
          works at all

which might be
                    that you
founder
            widening prior
measure of
                inform

found
        within
something
                sure
without
            something
shared

4/5

primacy in the following way
as well
          as one each more specific
each discordance from coral diffraction
to choral
             speciates and the host
of hopes among
                    the bride to lose to
want more than to
                      want unendingly

$$\frac{49}{60}$$

these mourning these nigh
all

   periods without
oddities in tow

               entreat
my self not thou
            enough

which cannot assuage

which can only absorb

you know all

                thoughs
about

       this nothing
this wants all I
have ever been once
beasts
            just run through

I am not I know
              wrong
you are caused
              a novelty
all despoliations
not power enough must
to stay
          commit all needs
coterminous
              to grace
that notion just crossed

$\dfrac{13}{15}$

compounds in
                mountains
religiously
            confound
abeyance by chance
                        Ø

it was so
            nice nice

$\frac{53}{60}$

the origins are
incessant the number

of presents
            no problem

the problem
              to long
in the wind
            assent

$$\frac{9}{10}$$

weak coupled to bending
vibrations for the worst

in order prepare
                a place
worse than
                pain it is

known prior as to whelm
nil
   coincident with

nostalgia is all
                jihad
frequent at the node

few of us are

bad as we feel
few of us are

good as we fcel
nobody thinks

this
	isn't fair

rosary of friends
                    bound
to collapse surely just
not fair
          weeping angles
innumerated
                    beasts
innumerable mass
like stars at the maw this

so called separates

a semblance of fulfillment
of the law is why
                    on earth
such as it is this time

for the rampant recurse
rejoin some
                how ever
how the thing lies
                    light on
the rock you may know not
who knows which
                    thing above
the blur and the blur of

mutable with in sight
hushed by the cloud
                    ahead
full of
        occultation
we are
            stardust inspirit
and infact
                delight
in this in
                ourselves in
infinite series
except
            the waves incense

the child who peoples
makes to
            devote the worlds

this weird enchantment

over the standard model
I rose and
            all enthralled

1

Acknowledgments and Notes

Versions of some of these have appeared in the following: *Hannah* (1.1.3); *Petri Press* (1.2; 1.4); *6x6* (1.3); *Ekleksographia* (1.5); *Union Seminary Quarterly Review* (1.6); *Esque* (1.7); *SET* (1.8.1, 3, 4); *LVNG* (1.8.2, 5, 6); *Weekday* (1.9).

Any influential source's words, phrasing, or thought from which I insufficiently swerve to claim comfortably as my own, regardless how obvious such may be, I hereby acknowledge and note:

George Gershwin and DuBose Heyward (1.1.1), William James (1.1.1; 1.6.11), Emily Dickinson (1.1.4; 1.7.1), John the Evangelist (1.1.7), Monsignor Lorenzo Albacete (1.1.7), Ralph Waldo Emerson (1.2.6), Robert E. Pollack (1.3.1), Walt Whitman (1.3.5), Hart Crane (1.3.5), Thinley Norbu (1.3.5; 1.6.7.2), Stéphen Mallarmé (1.4.6), René Magritte (1.5), Rock Forehead (1.6.3), Jim Jones (1.6.5), Jack Johnson (1.6.5), David Chaim Smith (1.6.7), Saint Augustine (1.6.7.1; 1.7.1), Exodus (1.6.7.1), T. S. Eliot (1.6.7.2), Nāgārjuna (1.6.7.2), Georg Cantor (1.6.7.2), Alec Schachner (1.6.8), Werner Heisenberg (1.6.9), Akron/Family (1.6.9), W. B. Yeats (1.6.10, 1.7.8), David Helfand (1.6.12.1), William Stafford (1.6.12.1), Ornette Coleman (1.6.12.1), Saint Francis (1.7.2), The Grateful Dead (1.7.2; 1.8.4), Brother Giles (1.7.2), Arthur Rimbaud (1.7.3), Ken Boothe (1.8.5), Al Brown (1.8.6), Emma Borges-Scott (1.9.1), His Holiness the 14th Dalai Lama (1.9.1), Erin Lothes (1.9.3), Ed Sortman (1.9.3), Paul the Apostle (1.9.3), Kay Redfield Jamison (1.9.5), Peter O'Leary (1.9.6), James Merrill (1.9.6)

Good Company

John and Martha Foley; Niall and family; Sue and Jim
Martens; Jay and Amy and their families; Agnes; Nick
Bainbridge; Rennie Bergstrum; Pat Brayton and Rob
Iverson; Kate Brummage; Lori Lanza, et al.; Tobi and
Danny McEnerny and family; Mike McGonigal; Matthew
Nienow and family; Lillium and Ted Pierson and family;
Erin Shafkind; Richard Kenney and Carol Light and family;
Daniel Lumley; Nada Oakley; Jefferson Community School;
The Schooner Adventuress; The Wooden Boat Foundation;
Salish Ocean Search and Rescue; Steve Bagley; Ali Beletic;
Rob Davis; Dana Janssen; Amy King; Dorla McIntosh and
Kevin Penton and family; Seth Olinsky; Chris Owens; Miles
Seaton; Dave Smith; Ed Sortman; Ryan Vanderhoof; Josh
Bell; Tim Donnelly; Greg Ford; David James Miller; Cynthia
and Charlie Peabody; Robert and Amy Pollack; Center for
the Study of Science and Religion at Columbia University;
Gimme! Coffee, Brooklyn; Ugly Duckling Presse; Rawaan
Alkhatib; Jae Choi; Rachel Fagnant and Joe Fassler; Dorian
Geisler; David Gorin; David Greder; Evan James; Leslie
Jamison; Emily Liebowitz; James and Vicki Longley and
family; Ayana Mathis and Nikki Terry; Hannah Sanghee
Park; Jen Percy; Steve Toussaint; Jean Fountain and
family; Dan Beachy-Quick; Jim Galvin; Mark Levine; Mel
Nichols; Geoffrey G. O'Brien; Peter O'Leary and family;
Janet Shepard; Rod Smith; Cole Swensen; Emily Wilson.
Jane Cramer. Emma Borges-Scott.

This list is not an exhaustive list, though making this list
has been exhausting. Many people have been kind to me.
I cannot give—I have not given—thanks enough nor to
enough, though I hope to have included most of those
who have given the most, whether material comfort or
psychic guidance or, as applies to most of the folks herein
and then some, some improbable combination thereof.
The low-probability event for which I am grateful is not so
much this book's becoming but that I am alive and alert at
all. Thanks, Everyone.